I0616226

TRIGGERED TO CHANGE

Overcoming a Life Full of Turbulence

JOHN CARTER

For more information, please emai directly at johncarter65477@gmail.com

ISBN: 979-8-89694-057-9 - eBook
ISBN: 979-8-89694-058-6 - Paperback

DEDICATION

I want to dedicate this book to Service Dog Project (SDP).

What an incredible charity. They raise and train Great Danes for the mobility impaired. Serving veterans, first responders and then the general public. SDP relies solely on donations and is going through a significant transformation. SDP is moving to another location. This is quite financially hard as they are building from scratch. This is why SDP is receiving 50% of profits from this book.

Knowing that another person who's fighting their challenge is going to receive an incredible Great Dane at no cost is heartwarming for me. Besides all the physical support, which is life-changing, they receive a very smart, loyal best friend.

Table of Contents

FOREWORD

When I first met John, I didn't know whether I could help him. He had come to the Granada House because, at the time, it was one of the first residential treatment programs for people in early recovery from substance use disorder who were also disabled.

John was using a wheelchair. I knew that wasn't a disqualifying problem because I had used a wheelchair once before re-learning to walk again. He also had a severe speech impediment. Nobody but me could understand his speech, so even though I was Executive Director, I became his counselor. I too had to overcome a severe speech impediment. I expected difficulties in getting him to meetings, because there weren't many AA meetings at that time that were accessible. But I had run into this before. Fortunately, other able-bodied residents volunteered to carry him in his chair down the stairs to church basements where meetings were held. What made me doubt that we could help John was his court case in Worcester. The charges against him were very serious, and the court system in Worcester was prejudiced against him. I knew he would probably spend time in prison, and that his chances of surviving that weren't good. To stay alive in his condition would be difficult, but to stay alive and sober would be a miracle.

But John is a person who believes in miracles, and for whom miracles are possible.

John built a strong program of recovery at Granada House. He participated in every aspect of the program, and his speech became better. He made friends among the residents and staff. He was admired for his courage, persistence and optimism.

I went with John to court and told the judge about his wonderful recovery. But the judge didn't care. He sentenced John to 10 years in prison. After John went to prison, I thought I would never see him again.

But I did see him again, and he was still in recovery! Not only that, but he was walking without the wheelchair, his speech was practically perfect, and he was out of jail! But he wanted to come back to Granada House. He said he wanted to reinforce his recovery and get a strong foundation for his life. During his second residency at Granada House, through hard work and to his joyful surprise, John found gainful employment and a foothold in society, and he graduated from Granada House.

Many years later, I ran across John in a restaurant, with his support dog Jagger. He told me he owned a gym in Brookline. He got great satisfaction in helping people get stronger, lose weight, improve their health and feel better. He had a great program of recovery, and his son was living with him.

John is a miracle. Faced with severe disability, active addiction and serious legal challenges, he fought back. He worked on recovering from addiction and disability, faced his legal situation and took responsibility.

I'm very proud to say John is my friend. I, for one, believe in miracles!

Deb Larson-Venable
In recovery
Proud ex-resident of Granada House
First disabled resident of Granada House

INTRODUCTION

Triggered to Change is about the many triggers in my life and how I changed as a result. A trigger is something that causes you to relapse, that is, go back to using alcohol or drugs. Triggering events can be internal or external. They all have life-altering consequences. This is a story of hope, resilience, humility and, most importantly, learning how to enjoy life and be thankful for the many good people who helped me along the way.

This story begins when I almost lost my life. I was shot in the head – my first triggering event, pun intended. That would only be the beginning, and, honestly, the easy part, as my life continued to spiral out of control with addictions and prison. Having "angels" by my side, I overcame all these obstacles and fears. Now I enjoy life. I am "playing it forward" as they say. I'm a personal trainer with my own private gym. My background helps me understand many of my clients' challenges of feeling helpless, being overweight, being differently abled, and having to face the seemingly insurmountable limitations society puts on you. This is why being a personal trainer and helping others is my calling.

One of the people who helped me was a client who convinced me to give a "TED Talk." It was an amazing experience! Getting a standing ovation was simply adrenaline-pumping awesome!

That's what motivated me to write this story. For a long time I kept doubting myself and putting it off. I dropped out of school in the eleventh grade and did not pay attention in the previous ten. Lord knows I'm no scholar, but I promise not to crash. So buckle up and enjoy the story of how I was triggered to change! And learn how Great Danes change lives!

CHAPTER 1

Gunshot

In this first chapter, you'll learn about the event that changed my life thirty-two years ago. Thankfully, my memory is intact and I can share this with you. Let's start.

It was a day I'll never forget – December 15, 1992, a day that nearly cost me my life – a day that certainly changed it. I'm not proud of this, but I was a muscle-pumped seventeen-year-old member of the Worcester Mafia. I thought I was Al Pacino in Scarface – or at least, I wanted to be Al Pacino. It started like most Tuesdays. I loved Tuesdays, as my job was collecting from people who lost in gambling the prior week. Wednesdays were not my favorite, as anyone who won in gambling for the week got paid on those days.

It was an extremely cold winter day. I was excited. I was to collect a large sum – $28,000 to be exact. My partner and I had arranged to meet our gambler client at 5 PM at his company. He owned a mechanic shop. He worked on large trucks and equipment. We arrived early, and there were customers in his shop.

I should have picked up on his lame excuse of "I forgot to bring the cash." Who would forget about owing bookies $28,000 and what it would mean not to pay up? I didn't notice how fidgety he was and his relaxed way towards the customers. He couldn't keep still, and wouldn't make eye contact. I guess I didn't notice, because I had my mind on the money, and thought I was indestructible. I was Al Pacino – Scarface!

The client asked if we would follow him to his house right down the street. Not thinking about it, we followed him to his home. It was a very large and nice house, but in a very isolated area. There were no other houses on the block. He led us through his garage. When we got through the dark garage to the door to enter the house, he said he needed to shut off the security alarm, and walked behind me. The last thing I remember, there was a gumball machine by the door and I wished I had a coin… then, BANG! I was down and blood was everywhere.

My partner, a very short, wiry Italian kid, was lucky enough to escape and call for help. The shooter must have thought I was dead, as I lay there in a pool of blood. I remember I came awake for a brief moment when the paramedics were attending to me. I thought I was being mugged, and I fought back. The paramedics told me months afterwards I was not moving. I was rushed to the local hospital. From there, I rode an air ambulance to a major hospital.

This client was a serious nut job! I learned later that this was his plan B. The police found a freshly dug ditch. He was a large equipment mechanic. If we had shown up on time, he would have capped us both, driven the car into the huge hole he had dug, covered it up, and called it a wrap! Our families would still be looking for us! He was scared. He owed more than he could handle, so he tried to eliminate his problem. He could have easily made a payment plan. I learned from watching Dad that a guy with a broken arm can't work and pay his bills, so it's better to give him some time to pay off his debts. This was good because, despite the way I liked to present myself, I couldn't hurt a fly!

I arrived at the hospital in critical condition. I remained in a coma for 90 days, and, well, to say the least, things got strange. This was the day my life was nearly lost, and it changed forever. You might think it was for the worse, but you'd be surprised! You might also assume things could never become more complicated, but they did – a lot more complicated. I'll explain how my choices brought me to my knees. But before I continue on with the story of heartache and pain prior to my recovery, I would like to give you a short glimpse back in time, and explain why I wanted to be a gangster.

CHAPTER 2

A Glance Back

I grew up in a world that evolved around family and love, how close a bond I had with my dad and how he tried to shield me from a world that I would eventually enter. How my childhood went from great and secure, to being tragically trashed at a very young age.

I'm John. I was born in Worcester, Massachusetts on May 2, 1968. I lived a very unconventional lifestyle. My dad was involved in organized crime – the Mob. My parents were very family-oriented, giving me a great childhood. I thank God daily that my memory is intact, so I can remember it all. I was the middle child of five. I had an older brother and sister and two younger brothers. Of the five, I was Dad's pet! I mean it seriously – he did not hide it!

I played every sport. I was a very good athlete, and Dad loved that. He would never miss a game! My dad was a family man. He absolutely loved his five kids and wife – and his parents, who lived right down the street. Supper was a very big deal for Dad. He wanted the family to eat together every night. I knew some day, when I was older, I also wanted to be surrounded every night by loved ones. My family owned a farm about a mile away from where we lived. It was awesome, with animals galore – goats, chickens, cows, pigs, and my favorite animal, horses. I had a horse my whole childhood. I loved going on long rides with Dad. These memories have always stayed with me, and never fail to bring a smile to my face. I really loved all animals. Growing up, my dream was to be a veterinarian, but those dreams were slowly drifting away at a very young age.

Dad took me to see Larry Bird and the Celtics win the title in 1984. He was always taking me to see his beloved Red Sox. He even took me to see U2 in concert. I greatly admired him. I loved him. He was my God! And that's why I wanted to be just like him!

He told me many times, he did not want me to get involved with his stuff. It didn't matter. I was already very much attracted to this lifestyle. I loved how others treated my dad with respect. Everyone went out of their way to please Dad. He never never had to wait anywhere. The respect was over the top. It was a total rush. It really attracted me. I was well on my way to becoming a hoodlum.

I was good at being bad, but I was still a good-hearted kid. I mean, I never wanted to fight. I got along with everyone. I hated violence, even though this was a big part of Dad's world. To be sure, Dad made sure it didn't become part of his home life, and his family was never exposed to violence. By being bad, I mean, for instance, when I was a junior in high school, I got into some mischief. The principal wanted to have a meeting with my parents. I had a woman friend who agreed to come to the meeting with me and pretend to be my mom. She should have won an Oscar!

When I was a sophomore in high school, I was the class loan shark. Borrow ten this week, pay me twenty next week. In my school, sports were huge. Every kid bet on football. I had a hundred kids betting on every game. My history teacher was my best customer! I loved the action and the lifestyle. I was fifteen and already had a Mustang parked in the driveway. I loved breaking the law and making money. All the cops knew my dad, so there were no consequences yet. I thought this would last forever, but things started changing rapidly.

I had no ambition to play sports anymore, even though I was very good. My grades were failing, because what was the point of school, anyway? Dad was busy doing his thing, Mom was busy with five kids – I flew under the radar. I had gotten my high school sweetheart pregnant. My dad taught me to "MAN UP." So that's what I did, and married her. At that point, who needs school? I dropped out. Now, things started to get really bad.

Dad got arrested by the FBI. My oldest brother was shooting heroin and was not doing well at all. My mom tried hard to keep it together, but she was overwhelmed. My marriage was already in trouble. I was always out running the streets and trying to be a gangster. I was not being a good husband or father. I was not Dad.

Dad received a ten-year sentence. After a few months in prison, things got worse. Dad got sick. At first, we had no idea just how bad. When I was told he was terminally ill with cancer, I was crushed! How could God let this happen?

The court had mercy for my dad, and pardoned him, setting him free. He was first sent to a hospital. He did not want to be alone at night in the hospital, so he asked me to stay with him. That made me feel so special – I mean, he wanted me! I could not believe this, my dad was a big strong man. He was six one and two hundred fifty pounds. He was the leader of the Mob and our family. He became an extremely fragile shadow of himself – an old, bedridden man. After a few nights in the hospital, he was sent home. My mom had his room set up like a hospital room. We took care of him until the end. Sometimes I wish my dad had not been so strong, and had given in sooner, as he suffered horribly. It seems such a horrible thing to think about! The day came when he took his last breath, and, although extremely sad, I was also relieved that he wasn't suffering anymore!

Dad was my hero, and that is why I wanted to wear his shoes. However, you just read, I was not his size. So in this chapter, you learned about my awesome upbringing in a loving family and growing up with entrepreneurial skills, although I used them in the wrong way at that time. It was not long after my Dad's passing that I was shot in the head, and my life went from bad to worse.

CHAPTER 3

The Dream

Apparently, you dream while you're in a coma. It was a very long dream, and it influenced me a lot. It was about how I almost quit, but that all was changed by a stranger who coached me to victory. After I woke up and realized it was not a dream, I learned about the grit and determination I would need to get stronger.

This dream was like life itself, but weird. I can remember the entire dream as if it was yesterday – the smells, the conversations, the people, etc. It was crazy. I was in a coma for ninety days and had one long dream. I dreamed I was alive in a hospital, but had no idea what was wrong with me. There were about a hundred patients in the room, and we were surrounded by a balcony staffed with cops. If we ever acted up or misbehaved, they would urinate on us. The disgusting smell is something I will never forget! The urine was so deep, the nurses had to wear wading boots, the kind used for fly fishing. They wore these rubber boots to bring us our food or medicine.

In my dream, we had a swim race every day. The winner got to go home. While going to the pool, I would feel pain. It got to be so bad and treacherous, that every fiber of my body screamed. I hated going in, but once I was floating in the water, the pain disappeared, and I could swim like a fish. This part of the dream made sense to me, as I had been on a swim team my entire childhood.

This race would happen daily, and I kept losing. After a while, I said, "That's it. I quit!" The pain and frustration were too much to bear anymore. I just wanted the pain to stop! So when it came time to go swimming and I refused to go, that was misbehaving, so I got drenched with piss. Then a man, whom I had never seen before nor who had any meaning to me, sat on the edge of my bed with an umbrella. He said, "You're not quitting, and I'm gonna coach you." Every day, for weeks, he took me to the pool to practice. Every time I would ask, "Why are you helping me?" He would just smile.

One day, the race was about to start. So my coach got me down to the pool, gave me a smile, and said, "Swim hard!" The gun went off, and the race started. I swam my ass off. Every time I came up to breathe, I saw my coach cheering me on. My hand touched the wall, I won the race – and my eyes opened!

I had lived. I had been given a 97% chance of dying, but I made it! The doctors had given my family little hope I would survive. A bullet had blown up in my brain. It had separated into nine fragments. Those fragments are still in my head to this day. Now, the hard work would begin – putting a life back together.

When my eyes opened, I was surrounded by my family. Everyone called my name. I could hear them, but I could not move or talk. My only communication was with my eyes.

While I was not able to move, I still had memory. At the time, I had no idea how valuable this would be. When I woke up, I guessed I had gotten mugged and cracked on the head by a baseball bat. Imagine my surprise to learn I had been the target of an execution!

This was where my road to recovery began. There was no way I was just going to quit! Dad taught me to keep fighting and never quit. I remembered I had wanted to quit the swim team. When Dad asked me why, I had answered not because of injury, which he would have understood, but because I had to be at practice at 5 AM. Dad explained that that was just bullshit. He would not let me quit! I always remembered this valuable lesson.

The first step to recovery was just sitting up in a recliner. This hurt like a million bolts of lightning going through my body. I hated it. My once big and lean muscles were dead. I couldn't even hold my head up. I felt useless and awful.

Over time, my neck muscles came back. I could see things improving with effort. This encouraged me to fight harder. I still could not talk. What I mean is, I made sounds that were meaningless. My speech therapist played a tape of me talking, but I couldn't understand it. Eventually, my speech started to become more understandable. The only area in which I was not getting any improvement was my left side. I still can't move my left side. I had been shot behind the right ear. That part of the brain controls your left side. Being right handed, it made a huge difference.

Once I was able to sit up, the next phase started – aqua therapy?! I couldn't believe they were talking about a pool. When I tried to tell them about my coma dream, they would just smile and move me along.

Aqua therapy was awesome! While in water, I had no fear of falling and getting hurt. I spent hours a day in the pool. Over weeks, I saw improvements. I could not believe how much progress I was making.

It was quite a moment when I could finally move my left arm and leg. Aqua therapy was working, and I was getting stronger. But I still had lots of limitations. As I said, I was lucky to have been shot on the right side. I remember my roommate Ted. Poor kid. Ted was eighteen when the van he was riding in smashed. His head went through the windshield. The front of his brain which controls memory was damaged. He could stand and walk around, but had no idea where he was. He did not know family. I couldn't move, but I knew I was in trouble. I was aware. How could Ted fix himself if he didn't know he was broken? After nine months, my hospital stay came to an end. My therapist said I was going to keep progressing as long as my drive stayed strong. I wish I had taken his advice, because my drive took me for a fucked-up ride.

In my crazy coma dream, a stranger would not let me quit. I believe in some way that he was Dad looking down on me. I was in a very deep hole, but I would not quit. You'd be surprised to see how far you could go to overcome life's challenges.

CHAPTER 4

Life After Hospital

Depression quickly overcame my life. I fed it with many different addictions. The cops eventually put an end to the madness!

I was super excited once I was discharged from the hospital. I returned to my childhood home. My sister now owned the house and welcomed me "home." Mom was now living in Florida. It was a two-story house, filled with many happy memories. There were also bad memories that would start to haunt me. Things started to get really bad.

After all the "welcome home" visits, all of which ended too quickly, I was alone in my wheelchair. That wheelchair represented all my limitations. It was a scary place. Depression hit. I was so scared of the future, I didn't know what to do. I started off eating my depression away. It felt good to eat, so I started eating everything. Soon I started drinking. One beer led to two beers, and so it began. It felt so good to get away for a while, to escape that wheelchair. If only I knew the price I would eventually pay…

Food and booze soon led to marijuana. Now I found myself in a predicament. I couldn't afford pot on top of my food and booze. I got in touch with an old friend and asked if he could help me out. That was how it started. I became a drug dealer.

My dad hated drugs. My oldest brother battled addiction his whole life. My dad tried and tried to help him, but nothing worked. This frustrated Dad greatly, as it was one problem he couldn't fix. I could only imagine how he would feel about me.

At first, I was a very small pot dealer. No one, including my sister, noticed what I was doing. My dealing covered my addiction to food, booze and pot. But I had to have more. I needed more to escape. I added cocaine to the mix.

The cocaine started with just doing one line. A friend was over who had it, I did it, and I was off. I don't think I took a day off from partying until the crash. A few days into this, I knew what I had to do to support this new habit, this new addiction. I made a call to my supplier and they were more than happy to assist. After a few weeks, I was not so little of a drug dealer.

Even being a full-blown addict, I was actually pretty good at being a drug dealer. Most people would have learned a lesson, being shot in the head, but not me. I got right back into this shit! Imagine, after going through an ordeal as bad as it was, deciding to become a low-life drug dealer in a wheelchair. It was not long before my dealing was noticeable, and the questions began. I knew this had to change, as my sister would kill me.

I got an apartment and set up shop. At first, things were going okay. I built a clientele of drug users, as I was always available. I found being reliable was essential to the business. Although my addictions were worsening, I was still able to function, and function well as a drug dealer. My old gangster was coming back. Now that I was very noticeable, I started selling small packages in my sister's basement. A year later, I'm moving big weight in my own apartment.

I was warned, as I grew up with a lot of folks on the side of the law. I was told I was under surveillance. My attitude was, "I don't care."

The way I saw it, I had to keep going. I mean, by then I weighed well over 300 lbs sitting in a wheelchair. Despite the weight gain, I was wasting away because I had done nothing for my body except fill it with junk food. I was a full blown addict. My life sucked so bad. I needed the food, alcohol, and mostly the drugs to escape the wheelchair. I had no choice!

Knowing I was being watched only made my addictions worse. I had to escape. I tried being more cautious, but I was deceiving myself. I was no match for the cops!

Then one day, I was sitting in my apartment partying by myself, watching Jerry Springer, when there came a "Boom!" Then the door crashed open. A dozen people all in black, wearing face masks, came barreling through. I thought I was dead. I thought I was being mugged. Then I heard a walkie-talkie, and I knew it was the cops.

I remember saying to myself, thank goodness – this shit is over! The cops searched the house. They found cash, cocaine, pot and pills. The police were very confused and couldn't understand why I was so easy-going and happy. My life was so badly messed-up that I didn't care what would happen. What I didn't realize, what I didn't know that day, was that my life was about to change for the better.

The cops felt bad for me and said, "We don't want to put a guy in a wheelchair in jail." The cops wanted me to wear a wire and set up my suppliers. They told me to pick up the drugs like I normally did, and not only would I not go to prison, but I wouldn't even have an arrest record. My response was quick – I already got shot once in the head, and didn't want to be shot again. I told them to just take me to jail, and they did. I was released on $10,000 bail. I was totally lost. I now weighed 330 pounds. I had no money, no drugs – and no escape.

My addiction took over my life. It filled me with shame, grief, and great sadness. I had become a drug dealer. I had become reckless. And now, the cops had me.

CHAPTER 5

Redemption: Prison and Halfway House

This was the turning point that would eventually allow me to build a lifestyle of happiness. First, I met a person who taught me how to deal with my many addictions. Second, a judge did me a favor, although, at the time, I didn't realize it. Third, inmates at prison taught me a trade that would turn into my passion. Throughout all of this, I remembered a lesson from Dad that kept me from making a horrible decision, which allowed me to start building a life.

After I was let out on bail, I was a broken mess. I didn't know what to do. I remember sitting in the police parking lot with a family member who suggested that I go to detox. Thank goodness I listened. To be honest, I really didn't have a lot of options. So, off to detox I went.

The first week, I was in a fog. When I came out of the fog, boy, did I hit a wall! I could not believe I had fucked up my life so badly. The depression and sadness were still there. The difference was, I was always with people. I was never alone, and it felt great. I wasn't the only one with problems. Soon after, I was accepted into a halfway house called Granada House. This is where my thinking and my life changed.

When I met the Executive Director, Deb, she came walking in with a limp. I could see she had challenges. During our meeting, she told me her story. It involved cocaine and a head trauma that nearly cost her her life. This confined her to a wheelchair for a while. I was so intrigued and inspired that she could walk now. I couldn't believe she actually did it, and put that damn chair out of her life! Being in a wheelchair is so horrific! I needed to escape the wheelchair.

She was so cool. She really cared, and it showed. I should say, what I meant by cool was, she drove a convertible standard Mustang. I wanted the happiness she had. I mean, she *glowed*! I listened to every word she said. Dad always told me, "when you're in the presence of someone who knows more than you, shut up and listen closely." So that's exactly what I did. Thank goodness! What a lesson! Thankfully, I was listening.

I started going to AA Meetings. I went to several AA meetings a day. I did what was necessary to keep sober. I had built a strong relationship with Deb. I really trusted and admired her. I felt very comfortable asking personal questions, as in, whether she had any regrets about not having children. She was well into her forties, and becoming a mother did not seem likely. She said, "Not in this lifetime. I'm busy getting and staying sober, working on my physical condition and building a life's work that I'm proud to have accomplished. Plus, you're all my children. I nourish and tend to you. I teach you how to live life and care for yourselves."

How true this would be for me. For without her teachings, I would not be here!

Deb and others emphasized to me that one has to work on recovery's physical aspect as much as its mental aspect. So, I joined the YMCA. It wasn't too far, and it felt wonderful to be independent. All I had to do was roll down the street. I still didn't need help. I was really loving the way I felt, but my problems were not disappearing just because I got sober. That would have been great, but that is not reality. It was time to face life on life's terms!

So the big day arrived when a court would decide my fate. I decided to waive the jury and hope that the judge would give me a second chance, seeing that I'd been sober and under Deb's care for nearly a year. So there I sat, in front of the judge with Deb and my lawyer by my side. I thought for sure the judge would be lenient, because this was my first offense, I was confined to a wheelchair, I had worked hard to get sober, and my character witnesses had said good things about me. My hopes were high and positive – but that quickly disappeared.

The judge looked down at me and said, "Mr. Carter, we don't discriminate in this courtroom. You're going to get the same punishment any drug dealing thug that comes through this courtroom in front of me would get." I knew this did not sound good. He proceeded to give me a ten-year sentence.

I almost fell out of my wheelchair. I couldn't believe this! I was a first-time offender in a wheelchair, and the judge was putting me in state prison with murderers. I was filled with anger. I was frightened, as I'd heard all the horrific stories about prison life. How was I ever going to get through this?

The judge was kind enough to give me a "stay of execution" for a week and let Deb transport me to prison. I really needed that week, as this was extremely emotionally difficult. Now, more than ever, I really leaned on Deb for support.

I remember riding home from court with her – the look in her eye and the tone in her voice. "John, you can run and hide, or you can man up and face your problems. Unless you face them, you'll never be happy," she said. So, obviously, off to prison I go. This phase of life would be a trip.

Talk about being scared! When I showed up at the state prison, I started to cry, just looking at the place. After the booking process, they kindly showed me to my new home. I was shocked. The cell was no bigger than a closet. They just wheeled me in, shut the big iron doors and left. I was totally alone.

I cried like a baby the first night. I was so angry and disappointed. I couldn't believe I had done this to myself. I started talking to Dad, asking him for help. I was down, and didn't think I could do this. Dad always taught me not to quit. I had no idea Dad was listening, because the next morning I got a welcoming visit.

Three guys entered my cell. I was petrified. They said, "Relax! We're friends of your dad, and we're going to help you." Wow! These were not guys I would associate with in my present life. Trust me, they met me with open arms! I learned that Dad had helped them in the past. I thought to myself, what respect! My dad was dead, but they were still looking out. Talk about a spiritual experience. Dad was looking out for me!

Being able to use the gym in prison was a huge privilege. Every chance we had, we took it. These three men taught me how to lift properly, how to modify my exercises, and how to improve them. Their intensity was unreal, and I loved it! I was getting stronger and stronger. More importantly, I was using that wheelchair less and less. What these men did for me, I cannot ever repay. I'll always be grateful. I mean, they did more for me than they know. I was an easy target inside, and they protected me. Boy, did they ever ease my mind and make my life so much smoother! I was beginning to see light at the end of the tunnel. I was amazed by how strong I was getting. I only had the ambition to train harder.

Well, the big day arrived when my friends entered my cell carrying a cane. They explained how they were taking my wheelchair and dumping it. I was very anxious, but with their help, I walked without fear and said goodbye to my prior life – to my wheelchair. That wheelchair had represented so much unhappiness in my life up to that point. We had a big celebration. It was not like the movies. We were able to eat together, and eat good food. My friends could cook using a hot pot. It was amazing compared to the jail food.

Jail really helped me physically, but mentally was another story. It was extremely challenging to look strong and solid, when I wanted to cry like a baby. For instance, my mom would bring my two daughters to visit. Watching them cry as they left at the end of the visit was the worst. I kept myself as busy as I could. I started running the AA meetings in prison. Staying busy really helped pass the time away. I studied for and earned my GED. I was so proud of myself! Now I could tell people that I got my degree upstate. I just didn't say prison.

One day, the guard came to my cell and sent me to the chaplain's office. I knew this couldn't be good. It was my ex-wife on the phone, telling me that my oldest brother overdosed and passed away. I couldn't move. I had only just talked to him the day before. Mom had been telling me about how bad his addiction was getting. I had pleaded with him on the phone to accept help, and do it right away. I had some good contacts, and he could have got help immediately. His excuse was that he needed a couple days to wrap things up. I tried to convince him, but unfortunately he wasn't ready. Please don't let this happen to you. If you're battling addiction, there is help. You might feel alone, but remember, you're not alone!

I want to emphasize how truly bad prison is. You lose all control. You're confined to a small cell with a lot of difficult people. Among other things, prison is filled with racism. The hate was over the top! I was surrounded by people who hated each other for no other reason than the color of their skin. Honestly, I think they just needed a place to direct their feelings of powerlessness. It was difficult for me to fit in. I had a very different mindset.

Let me explain. Most inmates get sober because of prison. I came to prison sober. None of them had any type of plan. They just couldn't wait to get released and return to their old ways. That was when it hit me. I had run into a guy I hadn't seen for months. I asked him where he had been. I thought he might have been in the hole (prison inside prison). He said they had let him out on parole, but he had violated it. This confused me. I couldn't believe he had been let out of this hell hole, but then chose to use drugs and come back. As he stood there grinning as if he didn't care, I thought to myself, what a fucking idiot! I mean, seriously, I couldn't stop thinking of this. I couldn't sleep, as this was really on my mind. Knowing this happens often (recidivism), I was determined not to let this happen to me. Lying in bed, I was really thinking of this, and I remembered a teaching from my dad – "fail to plan, plan to fail." Dad taught me many lessons. At that time, I realized I needed to make a plan, and who else could I lean on? So I called Deb.

She said, "I've been waiting for you to ask for help." So I made a plan to return to the halfway house upon my release. What an incredible teaching from Dad! Thank goodness I was listening, because, boy, was it a life saver! So now I had been an inmate for six years, and I was going in front of the parole board. The board was impressed that I had a plan for release. My parole was granted. I had another 5 weeks to serve. The inmates were shocked that I was going back to the halfway house without it being stipulated by the parole board. My answer was that I didn't want to spend my life in and out of prison.

Inmates that got a "slap on the wrist," never really learned from their mistakes. They went in and out of jail. This made me really start seeing that the judge, in retrospect, had done me a favor using tough love. Well, I don't think he loved me, but he was certainly tough. So I wrote a letter to the judge explaining my feelings. I wrote that I understood his point, that he was protecting his city. He actually wrote me back to wish me success.

So now comes my release. I had entered prison in December 1994. It was now December 2000. Again, this is not the movies. There was no nice car waiting for me. The prison gave me a hundred bucks, a train ticket, a ride to the station and a smart-ass officer who stood there grinning, saying, "See you soon!" Don't count on it!

So this is where I believe I made the decision that made the life I have now possible! I didn't take a left and go back to my old stomping grounds – I took a right and went back to the halfway house. I knew that my chances of survival if I returned home were close to zero. I knew I only had one option. Thank goodness my head was clear enough to hear the message from Dad. So I returned to the halfway house to rebuild my life.

Wow, was I flabbergasted! I could not believe how much things had changed – technology, cars, people! It was a whole new world. I was excited. So I got on the train to Boston. Deb had asked me to come directly to the halfway house. Although I had not had a drink in seven years, I was still very vulnerable. I returned and got a great big welcome. I got lots of praise for my hard work, as I was in so much better shape and condition. I was walking. My wheelchair was long behind me.

At that time, I couldn't put into words just how very strange I felt. Everything was different. Most importantly, I was not alone, and I really leaned on Deb for support. I wouldn't still be alive if it hadn't been for Deb and the halfway house!!

Now, the hardest work began – to stay out of prison. I had to get on the right track to happiness. This was extremely tough. This may seem strange to you, but for me, staying sober was so very much harder after coming back from prison, even though I hadn't had a drink in years. When I was at the halfway house the first time, my only concern was staying sober and working on my health. Obviously, I had to do those things – I had no choice, and I loved getting stronger. Now, I had to learn how to live life on life's terms, and with all the temptations.

I had a lot to be proud of and very thankful for. I went from weighing over three hundred pounds and confined to a wheelchair, to two hundred five pounds and walking. I had a hard time walking.

The bullet destroyed many parts of my brain. Seriously, there's an empty space inside my skull. The bullet destroyed the labyrinth in my inner left ear. I cannot hear out of that ear, and have difficulty walking because of this injury. My speech also slurs terribly because of the brain damage. What's worse, there are still fragments from the bullet in my brain. So if I fall, it could move these fragments and cause more damage to my brain. I was still having trouble mentally, aside from the damage in my brain. Deb helped me there. With all her support, suggestions, and willingness to listen, Deb got me through this difficult time.

Deb strongly suggested that I work. There's a very busy intersection near the halfway house called "Harvard Square". There are hundreds of businesses in this location. At Deb's suggestion, I started looking for a job. I knew this was not going to be easy given my physical challenges and being an ex-con. To my surprise, I got hired on my first try! I started standing on the sidewalk selling newspapers and magazines. I made 7 bucks an hour and was happy as a pig in shit. I mean, I had just come from a prison job, making fifty cents a day. I was so extremely grateful, and Deb always reminded me that I needed to humble myself.

So I still had issues, but I started to feel better about myself. My job was a 30-minute walk away, and my starting time was 5 AM. The boss was extremely strict, and made it very clear that my first day late would be my last. Trust me, I was always early.

Every morning while walking to work, I had to cross a bridge over the Charles River. I would always stop. At 4:30 AM, there was no sound except the river. It was so peaceful. I always arrived early so I could stop and enjoy the fresh scent, and give lots of thanks to my higher power. I was loving life and becoming happier each day! I was determined not to let this happiness end. The only thing I knew that would continue to make this possible was to just not have that first drink! I couldn't understand relapsing – you build your life up and gain happiness, only to have it all come to an end – just for a drink?

My parole officer was so impressed with my work ethic and desire to stay out of prison. He would stop by the newspaper stand occasionally. He never gave a drug test. After some time passed, I asked him why he had never tested me. He said, "No need. It's obvious you want to be free." That's why I would listen and do the work necessary to stay sober. I wanted to be free, I really had no animosity towards anyone.

I remember going to the gym one day and finding one of the cops that had busted me also working out. I couldn't believe it! He didn't recognize me. I was sure it was him. He had been friendly with my Dad. I had always seen him while I was growing up. I approached him. We had a great conversation. I thanked him. I let him know how I felt. I'd been a low-life drug dealer, and getting busted saved my life. Everything was coming together – mentally, physically and emotionally. I was loving life.

I knew selling newspapers for a living was just not going to cut it. Although my passion for health and fitness training had not yet emerged, I'd learned how helpful the gym was for me both mentally and physically. I give many thanks to the inmates who helped me. Who would have thought I'd go to prison and be taught a valuable lesson by convicts? So I set out to be a trainer and help other people find their way.

I'll always be grateful for Deb. God always seems to put "superheroes" in my life. I was taught to face life, although I wanted to hide. My dad sent me help when I was alone and petrified. I was so grateful for my first job – it gave me the ambition to want more.

CHAPTER 6

Titanium Was Born

My frustrating job search turns into happiness with persistence. Training is my passion. How lucky I was when I met my first client. The birth of Titanium Health and Fitness was my dream come true.

So now I was determined to find a trainer's job. How would I do this? Aside from my newspaper job, I had never applied for a job. I thought applying in person would be the best course for me. I made a list of the local gyms, and set off on a mission. It didn't take long for frustration to set in. Everywhere I looked, no one would give me the time of day. I slurred terribly, and couldn't walk a straight line. They didn't believe I could do this. My frustration was becoming overwhelming. Thankfully, I was learning from Deb and all the positive people in my life. This helped me to keep pushing forward!

A friend asked me to go train with him, so I did. It just so happened the gym he went to was on my list of gyms to apply to, but I had not done that yet. So I said to myself, maybe I will apply. The only difference was, whenever I applied for a training job, I'd go dressed as you would to go to a job interview. This time, I was in my gym clothes. But I did have a good physique, thanks to prison. My awkward gait was not so apparent, given the muscles and little body fat. I spotted the manager. He was about 5' 10" and built like a fire hydrant – intimidating! But as I watched him, I learned how friendly he was. He greeted everyone with a smile, and was extremely welcoming. I waited for a chance, and it finally came. I saw him alone, so I built up my confidence and went for it. Thank goodness I walked through my fear and approached him! I introduced myself and said, "I'm looking to be a trainer." He replied, "I have a few minutes."

We went into his office, and the few minutes turned into over an hour. At the end of the long conversation, he said, "Can you start tomorrow?" I almost fell over. I couldn't believe this. He handed me the application, and I realized I had not yet told him I had been in prison. This is where it became tricky. I said to myself, "Fuck it!" and told him the story.

Thank goodness I did, because he was so understanding. He said just don't answer that question and this application goes no further than this room. I was overwhelmed with gratitude. I think I did a backflip!

That night I got a phone call from my new boss. "My morning trainer just called in sick, and I'm an hour away. Can you open the gym? Immediately, I said, "Of course!"

After I spoke, I realized I had no clue how to do this. He told me the combination to get in and all the things I had to do, like turn on the lights and greet people. I couldn't believe he was trusting an ex-con with the combination to his gym!

So I got to the gym at 5 AM and opened it up. I was so excited! By 6 o'clock, the gym was busy. A guy walked in and asked for the guy that called in sick. He was a new customer and had booked a training session. I explained he was out, but I could help. We went into the office and I learned what his needs were.

He was in his fifties, overweight, and not in the best health. He had many problems – diabetes, ankle, knee, back, neck, etc. I was overwhelmed by his list of problems, but I didn't show it. We proceeded to the gym floor, and I gave him a very light workout. We talked a lot about health. Obviously, he knew something had happened to me. My gait and speech were obvious. I just replied that I had been in an accident, and left it there. He was super-impressed with the fact that I had lost over a hundred pounds and was able to build my body up.

When his training ended, we went back to the office. This was where I was supposed to sell him on a training package and make him my first client. We had menus with the different session packages and prices, so I handed that to him. He looked at it for a few minutes, then said "I'll take a fifty package." I thought I heard him wrong, as that cost $4,500. I could not believe this was happening! I had no clue what to do next. That's when my boss came into the gym. As soon as I saw him, I excused myself and I ran to him.

"I need help, this guy wants to buy a fifty pack," I said to my boss. He told me to stop kidding, and then he noticed I was serious. He told me to just follow him. We went into the office and I watched his magical way of closing the deal. After the new client left, my boss and I sat and chatted. He taught me that being a trainer is great, but you have to be a good salesman also. You can be the best trainer in the world, but if you can't sell yourself, you'll become a broke trainer. My boss then told me that he had just started the fifty pack deal two weeks ago, and I had made the first sale! Talk about the first day on the job!

My boss told me that I had a lot of potential – that I had a very intriguing story that could inspire and motivate people trying to get healthy. That was the start. That month, I was the company's number 1 trainer. I brought in more revenue than anyone, including the boss! I quickly became his favorite. I felt great!

I asked him why he had given me an opportunity in the first place. He said it was because I had a very unique story. Life had been challenging for me. Besides, everyone deserves a second chance. Also, his mom passed after battling addiction for years. He wished she could have had a chance to talk with me. He liked the fact I was straightforward about prison. It showed I was honest, so he felt he could trust me. Wow, was I speechless! Being honest and forthright about your life and past can really resonate with people.

So now I was off and running. I had built up a nice clientele. This all came naturally to me, and I was thriving. My clients really were inspired and motivated by me. I loved it, as I was very motivated to help. This is where I believe my passion showed. I loved being in the gym, and absolutely loved motivating and helping people, especially people like me with challenges.

Now my boss was leaving the company to open his own gym, and it was not long before I got his call asking me to join him. Without hesitation, I went with him. It was quite a change, coming from a big gym to a small private gym. Most of my clientele followed me, and I was doing well at marketing. I mean, I'm selling health, not used cars. It was at this point that Titanium was born.

My boss decided to get married and leave the state. So I had two options – get another job, or buy him out. I chose to buy him out, and boy, was this tough! I didn't have much money, but I knew I could make it work. I scratched and saved. I had a friend who believed in me and was willing to help, so I accepted. Thank goodness!

I always wanted to be my own boss. I couldn't believe I had the chance to own my own gym as well. Was this really happening? Was it possible? Thanks to sobriety, the answer was yes.

I'd always been a hustler and entrepreneur – even as a child, and I knew I could do this. When I was young, like ten, my crew and I ran the neighborhood. Every driveway and yard were ours for the taking – snow shoveling, mowing lawns, you name it. The good thing about it was, we had no competition. I mean, no kid would dare to shovel in our territory. I had more money in the bank then than I do now.

I went to a catholic school where the nuns were extremely strict. We were required to have a pencil, pen, ruler and tie in every class. If you didn't, you'd receive a detention. Trust me, you would rather have a root canal than spend an hour after school with a mean old nun. So I filled my duffel bag with pencils, pens, rulers and ties to rent them to all the kids. There was a line at my desk every morning. I was the richest kid around.

Starting the gym was real life. Initially, I couldn't afford to pay two rents, so I sent my three-year-old son, who had been living with me, to my sister's, and moved into my new gym. Even doing this, I didn't have much money left. I think I had eighteen bucks! All the same, I was extremely happy and proud of myself. After being released from prison and in my condition, I now owned my own gym. I was so happy and full of energy.

Part of my happiness came from using the skills I had learned as a younger kid. When I was young, I used them for the wrong reason. Now, I was using these skills as a successful entrepreneur. I loved it. I was there all the time. It felt like I lived there. Wait a second – I did at first!

My first problem with my own private gym was a personal one. In the last gym, the setting was much bigger with lots of people. So when a client asked what happened, I could easily sidestep the question. Now, my gym, while spacious, is smaller and private. Sidestepping the question was not an option. So I spinned my story so as not to lie. I'd say, "I was in a hunting accident and got shot in the head." Actually, it was very truthful – I just left out the part where I was the one being hunted! I mean, I'm trying to sell myself. Imagine me saying, "I was involved with crime, got shot in the head and went to prison. But write me a check." They would run!

This allowed me time to build relationships. Only when that was established, would I tell them the full truth. People couldn't believe it. I mean, you can't make this shit up! The positive reaction I received gave me the confidence to open up and tell my story.

Once, I had just started to train a new client. After some time, I really started trusting her, and would tell her bits and pieces of my story. After a month of sharing, she said that was an amazing story that needed to be told. She had contacts with people involved with TED talks. She scheduled a meeting for me. When I walked out of the meeting, I was like WTF! What did she get me involved in? There was no way I could do this (or so I thought).

She asked me to trust her. So I walked through my fear, and did it. Thank goodness! Doing that TED talk was awesome! The adrenaline was a rush. I felt like I was playing football again. I loved talking, and that gave me the confidence to write this story.

My clients are awesome. They are my network of friends. I absolutely love this! I hear people say how unsatisfied and unhappy they are with their work. I love my work! I can't wait to get back to my gym. When my alarm goes off at 4 AM, my body never wants to get up. I say to myself, "Carter, get your ass up! You have obligations." I love it when a client sees progress. I love how awesome it feels when my clients start reaching their goals. I've had several clients lose over a hundred pounds. I know this is life-changing for them. It's so rewarding to help change someone's life. I've had several severely injured clients make unbelievably healthy gains. I believe that because of my background, because I'm differently abled, because I got out of that wheelchair and lost all that weight, I can now pay it forward and help others.

I ran into an old client I had not seen in years. He looked great! I said, "It's great to see you kept up the hard work." He quickly reminded me that I always say, "There are 168 hours in a week. How many of them do you dedicate to your health?" He said dedicating time each week to working out changed his life. My clients are quite diverse – young, old, male, female, gay, straight, injured, differently abled, or just trying to get healthy. They love the privacy of my gym. It allows them to feel comfortable, safe, and able to train hard. And do they love to see Turbulence, my Great Dane service dog! He weighed two hundred pounds and was a gentle giant. He especially loved it when my clients brought treats.

I had been in business now for eleven years. In December 2019, a better space opened up in my building, so I moved. I hired a contractor, bought new state-of-the-art equipment, and really designed an awesome gym. My clients loved training in the new space, and I was so very happy. Then, out of the blue, came Covid. I had just invested my entire savings on constructing a new gym. I went from fifty hours a week to zero overnight. It was crazy. I thought I was so fucked! Talk about stress! But it turned out okay. Thank goodness my gym was private! Because my gym was private, people who didn't want to go to their public gym started seeking me out, and my business started thriving again. People felt they could train safely in my gym.

My equipment is very diverse, and I designed a very unique gym. I can train the elderly or an Olympian. I really enjoy training couples – spouses, parents, siblings, etc.

A manager at a gym gave me a second chance that would mold my future. From signing my first client, I gained much-needed confidence to get my second. I opened my own gym, and things came together because I did the work to stay sober.

This next phase of life would bring great joy!

CHAPTER 7

Service Dog Project (SDP)

When I found the Service Dog Project ("SDP"), my life changed so much. This special charity fills recipients with lots of happiness by supplying them with specially trained Great Danes. My first dog was Jagger until he retired and passed the torch to Turbulence ("Turby"). These dogs help me walk and get around, freeing me to travel.

In 2019, I watched a program about service dogs for the mobility-impaired. Obviously, I was very interested. With advancing age, my balance was really deteriorating. I'd occasionally use a cane. I hated the cane because it was totally useless for preventing me from falling, which was occurring more frequently. Remember, the metal pieces in my brain could still shift and cause serious damage in a fall, not to mention the horrors of falling, not being coordinated enough to stop it, and breaking or badly bruising something. I was getting older and really starting to fall too often.

I did some investigating, and thank goodness, I found SDP. I'll never forget how SDP brought so much joy into my life! What a fabulous charity! They raise and train Great Danes for the mobility impaired. They give the recipient a Great Dane free of charge and primarily cater to veterans and first responders. This place is special. After all, my life was saved by first responders.

Every Sunday they have an "open house." When I went, they graciously greeted me and gave me a tour of the farm. I was amazed! The litters are generally named according to a theme. When I was there, the talk of the farm were the "rock stars" – Bowie, Jagger, Elvis, etc. If you had known me as a kid, you'd know that I was a huge Rolling Stones fan. Mick Jagger was and still is my idol!

When I met Jagger, I instantly fell in love. At that time, Jagger was six months old. I prayed to receive Jagger, but the odds were against it. SDP doesn't tell you what dog you'll receive. They do their own analysis and match you with the appropriate dog. There were 60 dogs on the farm, so getting Jagger seemed unlikely.

I got on their waiting list. My son and I volunteered there to learn more about this great organization. Every Sunday we'd commute there by train. Being there made me feel so happy!

When it's your turn to receive a dog, you have a final meeting with SDP so they can learn about your daily life and specific needs. They do this so they can properly train and fine-tune your dog. When it was my turn for the interview, they learned that I was basically a city boy. I was always on and off the trolleys.

Sunday rolled around, and off to SDP we went. I asked another volunteer where Jagger was. He said he was in the barn, and that this would probably be the last time I'd see him. "Why?" I asked nervously. He said because some lucky SOB from Boston had been matched with him. I was getting really good at backflips! They were training him to get on and off the trolleys. This could not be true – could it? A week later, I got the news that I had been matched with Jagger.

SDP has a requirement. The dog needs to bond with the recipient before the recipient can take him home. They have a guest house on the farm. You come and stay a few nights with the dog. It was now my turn. I was overwhelmed with joy! The trainers explained to me that the dog was content right now. Once Jagger realized his trainers weren't there, he would get upset. Oh boy, once Jagger noticed the trainers had snuck out, his anxiety was over the top! Jagger ran from window to window looking for them. Although I'd known him for a year, now he still wanted his trainer and nothing to do with me. The next morning the trainer came by the house to take us out for some training. When I told her about the trouble we were having with bonding, she told me that if we didn't bond, they'd have to try another dog. They couldn't let me take Jagger home unless Jagger was happy with the change. Wait. What? I said to myself. "No fucking way!" Jagger had been in my heart for over a year. I wasn't leaving without him. So when we got back to the house, Jagger and I had a face to face.

Around midnight, I was watching TV. Jagger was on his bed in front of me. When Jagger got up to get a drink, I realized this was the perfect time to act. I got down and laid on his bed. Jagger turned around and gave me this funny look, like "WTF?" I looked at him and said, "Sorry, buddy, I'm not moving!" After a few minutes he came and laid down and let me pet him. After about an hour, I got up and went to my bed. It wasn't long before he climbed onto the bed and put his big head on my chest. It was over. He was now my best friend.

I knew that coming from his farm home to the city was going to be quite a relocating process. I mean, he came from hearing roosters and cows, to noisy trains, buses, cars, etc. Jagger was very nervous, but he trusted me. Our bond was so tight! Jagger became the rock star of my town. Everyone was amazed, and Jagger definitely loved the limelight! I think some people joined my gym just to get to hang out with Jagger. He has been in our local newspaper twice, and won the most-read article!

Talk about a godsend – when Covid hit, he was my savior! I mean, I had enough mental health issues. Adding being alone would have put me over the top. Jagger was always there, and kept me going.

Unfortunately, after only two years, Jagger got severely ill with a blood disorder. We almost lost him, but Jagger was a fighter. With the help of SDP and all the angels who helped on a GoFundMe page, we were able to save his life. Although I had to retire him from my service, I didn't realize at the time he would become my mom's best friend. SDP stepped right up to assist me – thank goodness – because now I have Turbulence. At a massive 198 lbs of muscle, Turby is quite the attraction. I can't express how grateful I am. Turbulence is now my new best friend. I'm with him twenty-four hours a day. Our bond is very strong. Great Danes are an amazing breed, and SDP does a superior job of training!

My daughter and her family live in Florida. I planned a long promised trip to visit her, but I was so very nervous. I mean, flying with a two hundred-pound Great Dane did not seem easy. Right away, Lynn, the president of SDP, stepped right up. I took Turby back to the farm. Lynn had simulated the inside of the airplane and trained us. What a great job, as the way Turbulence had learned to move his body was awesome. I reserved three seats. He backed in with ease, and took the whole row. To be honest, I was so nervous for myself. I mean, I have trouble going to the back yard, never mind going to Florida alone. But I was not alone – I had Turby! He was unreal! What a sight! People were amazed!

Turbulence never left my side. Nothing distracted him – not the busyness of the airport, nothing! Boarding the plane was a trip! During the flight, the pilot on the intercom announced, "Folks, we have some *turbulence* on board that we can't get rid of…". He then laughed and pointed out that Turbulence was the name of my stability dog. The shocked passengers then laughed and became very friendly.

Turby opened up the world to me. He taught me that I can go anywhere. What a great lesson!

I've met quite a few people waiting to get matched with their helper. SDP is a volunteer-run farm, and most who are waiting to be matched, volunteer. While my son and I were up at the farm doing work, I watched the dogs play with this young kid. I think he was 12, and he had MS, I believe. He walked with crutches. He asked me if I thought they would give him a dog. I said, "Buddy, it's not *if*, it's *when*." Shortly after that, he was matched. I didn't know him at all, but I'm sure he's loving life now! Can you imagine walking down your school corridor with a Great Dane who weighs more than you? What a sight! That's why the final meeting before you're matched is so essential. They tailor your dog to your specific needs. They change lives!

I remember one day up at the farm, Jagger was in the kennel. So I went to say hello to him. There was a gentleman already visiting Jagger, so I introduced myself. It turned out he was a veteran that had returned home from Afghanistan. He had suffered a traumatic brain injury that caused balance issues. We talked, and he said, "Jagger is my favorite, and I pray I get him." At first, I was very hurt, as I wanted Jagger for myself. But then my feelings changed. I thought to myself, this guy is a hero and deserves what he wishes. He was later matched with a different dog. In the end, he couldn't go wrong, as every dog on the farm is totally incredible!

I can go on forever about how great SDP is. Hundreds have gone through the process of getting matched. They have the incalculable joy of meeting their best friend! And I did it twice! I can't say it enough – they change lives!

SDP is a magical place. Recipients receive not only a service dog, but a best friend. Words cannot express how grateful I am. Thank you, SDP, for all that support, and make the next recipient's life so much happier!

CHAPTER 8 EPILOGUE

My Life Today

Turning my life around allowed me to build the family I always wanted – the close relationship I have with my son, the courage to follow my dad's wishes and the ability to take care of my mom. My battles are far from over, especially the constant pain caused by drugs. I have adapted, accepted myself, and flourished.

So here we are in 2024. Like everyone, my life has had its ups and downs. I love my life. I'm a family man. I might not have much money, but I'm wealthy with love. I have two incredible daughters, one awesome son, three amazing grandsons, one beautiful granddaughter, two Great Danes and a small cat.

I told you how I lost my older brother to a drug overdose while in prison. Recently, I lost my youngest brother Russell to an overdose of fentanyl. Russell was the family favorite – so filled with life and the ability to make everyone around him happy. Did I tell you I hate drugs? Addiction brings nothing but pain and chaos, especially to the family of the addict!

My daughters are super moms! My oldest daughter Brianna lives in Florida with her husband David, sons Ethan and Cash, and the princess Elle Rose. Brianna takes after her dad – she's an entrepreneur and owns a skincare salon. My second daughter Nichole lives in Worcester, Massachusetts with her son Julius. She's a registered nurse, studying to become a Nurse Practitioner. This profession suits her well, as she has such a kind, gentle heart. Although I missed most of their childhood while I was on drugs and in prison, we have a very tight bond. They have graciously forgiven me. In fact, they never made me feel worse than I already did. Being a dad was my obligation, and I failed! It took me a long time to forgive myself. To say I'm proud of them, is an understatement! My ex-wife and family did a great job installing moral skills, and now they are raising incredible families of their own.

I live with my son and my eighty-one-year-old mom who has dementia. My sister lives with us to help us. She's a saint. Without her, I wouldn't have been able to achieve my goal of keeping my mom out of the nursing home. This really means a lot to me, as one of my last talks with Dad was about my looking after her – and I promised I would.

My mom had my back my entire life. I want to be there for her even now. Mom has moments of clarity. Last night, as I was tucking her in, she said, without any confusion, "Thanks for taking care of me." Instantly, I said, "Thanks for being my Mom." I cried with joy, as it was an honor to be by her side. I know my dad would be very proud of this! And to think I made Dad proud of me!

One day you might have the privilege and honor of caring for someone who always cared for you. Earlier, I told you about Jagger. He became my mom's service dog. They both need each other. My mom became Jagger's nurse when Jagger was injured. Fortunately, all that time, my mom was physically able to assist Jagger. Her love and pampering made Jagger so happy, and he had a successful recovery. Now he returns the favor and takes care of my mom. He keeps her company and makes her laugh. They are together twenty-four hours a day.

What a match! For example, my mom's emotions are sometimes overwhelming. Whenever she gets depressed, she sits in her wheelchair and starts crying. It's hard for us! Jagger gets right up, puts his big head on her lap and looks into her eyes. My mom stops crying and gives Jagger love! It is really painfully hard to see Mom suffering in a wheelchair like I did. Thank goodness for Jagger!

My son Matthew is nineteen, and one awesome son! The help he does for our family is invaluable. I never hear a negative word from him – seriously, never. And I'm always leaning on him for help. Every day, when I wake up early for work, I always call Matthew to take the dogs out and help me. I never hear anything besides "Coming Daddy" – and, I'm talking 4 AM for the last decade.

Matthew is off to college this year, and I'm already missing him. Only yesterday, I was walking Matthew to kindergarten. He's now a delightful, kind young man, off to college. Life is just so fast, but it is awesome! We've been side by side for nineteen years, and he's my right-hand man. When he goes away for a weekend, I'm lost without him. I'm glad he's going to college – Matthew needs to live *his* life, not mine! He's going to major in biology because of his interest and love for science. He loves animals, and wants to become a veterinarian.

One of my biggest regrets was not going to college. Remember, I told you about my first job after release from prison, selling newspapers in Harvard Square. Well, right across the street was Harvard University. Every morning, I'd watch all the kids gather, and wish I'd chosen that life. Now, Matthew's going to let me live my dream through his eyes. What a blessing!

When Matthew was a junior in high school, his goal was to work at McDonald's so he could eat all the Big Macs. This changed when he became a senior. Then, his goal was to become a YouTube gamer. I thought it would be better if he took a gap year. That worked, because now he's off to college. Did I tell you how proud I am?

Matthew not only helps with the dogs, he's a big part of taking care of his grandmother. I explained to him that one day that will be me. I don't just want a room in your apartment, I want my own wing with a swimming pool, jacuzzi, and sauna. I didn't think he could swing that on a McDonald's paycheck.

Matthew has had his own difficulties which have made him very strong. His mom passed away during the Covid pandemic. It was a very difficult time for him, as they were so very close. I know she was extremely proud of him.

You've met Turbulence and Jagger. Please allow me to introduce Mick the cat. When we first took Jagger home, we knew he needed a friend. Matthew had been asking for a cat, so I figured this was a perfect time. I did mention I'm a huge Rolling Stones fan, so naming him was a no-brainer. This little kitten, no bigger than Jagger's head, is named "Mick". What a great cat. Mick has to deal with two Great Danes. They're all best friends. It's so funny to watch a three-pound cat bossing around two, two-hundred-pound Great Danes.

At first, when Turbulence entered the picture, Jagger didn't want to give up his role as a service dog. He finally gave in and passed the torch. This was tough for Jagger, as he's a very proud dog. Great Danes love working and helping their master.

Things are not always nice and easy. Being sober, I'm able to face life on life's terms and create a very friendly, happy home. I'm usually cheerful. I'm with someone new every hour at work, and I work with them to improve their body composition and their lives. I really enjoy being with people. I love my profession. I was asked by a long term client, "How can you always be so cheerful after what life has taken from you?" My answer was swift, "Life has given me much more than it has taken!" I've tried to make amends to all the people I'd ever hurt, and forgiven all those who'd done me wrong. I've forgiven the man who shot me years ago. I was taught that I must forgive if I want true happiness. This is very hard, but very true. When I think about what happened, I really don't have animosity towards the shooter. I knew what I was involved in. It's not like I was crossing the street and got hit by a bus – I was playing with fire and got burned.

Writing this story has brought lots of tears and smiles. Thank you so much for reading and supporting SDP. I did warn you that I'm not a scholar. I wanted to share my story and not have it come from an author. I hope this book inspired you in some way. Whether it's food, gambling, alcohol, drugs or some other addiction, you're not alone. For myself, being alone brought on depression and sadness. If you're in this situation, please get help so you can avoid all the pain and inflicting pain on those you love. If you're at that young age in life, think really hard about that choice you're about to make, because it may save you from a world of hurt. You are not alone!

If you've suffered an injury or faced hard times, dig down deep, have faith and learn to trust. If you do the work, things will get happier! You just learned what I did. You can do it as well. No matter what your fight is, keep fighting, walk through your fears, and eventually, you will find happiness waiting for you.

Thanks,
John

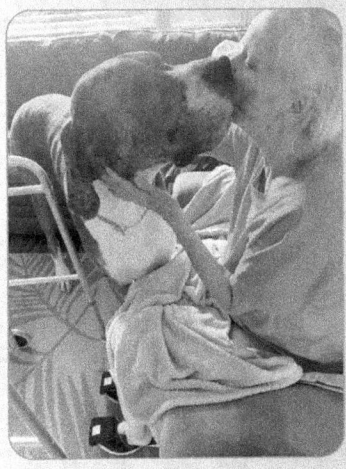

Turbulence and my mother

Me before and after

Jagger

Jagger and my mother

Me and my son Matthew

Turbulence

Me and my 2 dogs

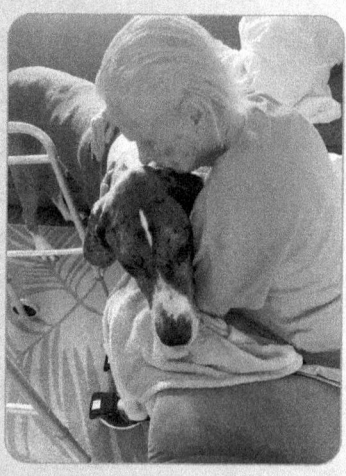

Turby and mom again

Me and my 2 dogs again

Turbulence and Jagger

**Brother Michael
and I visiting Dad in
Federal Prison**

Jagger in his prime

ACKNOWLEDGMENTS

As I sit here writing my acknowledgments, it happens to be October fifteenth, twenty-four, thirty years since my last drug. I would like to thank the man upstairs. Whenever I need a helping hand you always inject an angel in my life and concerning sobriety, it was Deb. Without her none of this would be possible. The lessons she taught me were invaluable. The strength she showed me I had to fight and face my challenges allowed me to become the man I am today. This was my first " trigger to change "and for that I'm forever grateful!

I would also like to thank my son Matthew. It's awesome being your dad, you make me extremely proud. My two daughters, Brianna and Nichole. Watching you two be moms is incredible. My grandchildren are so fortunate to have you as their mom.

Lynn and the whole service dog project family, For all the lives you change, starting with mine.

Jagger and Turbulence, not only for all the physical support, but for all the love you brought into my life.

My clients who make my day awesome. Watching your dedication for a healthy lifestyle is remarkable.

My friends, I can't thank you enough. I know I'm needy and you guys are always willing to lend support and help. I am forever grateful!

Concerning this book Jamar who gave my story a title. Timmothy, Deb, Richard, Lynn, and my son Matthew, without your help this project , which was extremely hard for me, would of been impossible.

I believe God puts people in your life for a reason. And for me that's been happening my whole life. Seriously, whenever I'm in need he puts an angel in my life.

I am such a blessed man!

And finally, a special thanks to all who support S.D.P

AUTHOR BIO

JOHN CARTER is a personal trainer, motivational speaker, and owner of Titanium Health & Fitness, a private gym in Boston. After surviving a near-fatal gunshot, battling addiction, and enduring the trials of prison, he rebuilt his life and found purpose in helping others overcome their own challenges. Through his fitness programs and speaking engagements, John inspires others with his story of resilience, healing, and transformation. *Triggered to Change* is his first book, sharing his journey from despair to empowerment and the power of second chances.

BOOK PROCEEDS

The Service Dog Project (SDP) is a non-profit 501(c)(3) charity that provides Great Dane mobility service dogs to individuals with mobility challenges. The organization was founded in 2003 and has donated over 170 service dogs. These trained Danes are committed to helping their partners achieve greater independence and improve their overall quality of life. We cater to veterans, first responders and then the general public.

Volunteers complete the majority of the work done at the organization. Community service hours are provided for students from numerous schools around us. We are always looking for dedicated volunteers to help us achieve our mission of providing service dogs to those in need. As a volunteer with SDP, you will have the opportunity to make a real difference in someone's life. No matter your skills or interests, we have opportunities for everyone to get involved and make a meaningful impact. We rely on grants, donations, and fundraising so we can continue to donate our dogs at no cost to those who qualify.

Learn more at:https://www.servicedogproject.org/

To help support this vital mission, **50% of the profits from this book will be donated to the Service Dog Project (SDP).** This contribution will help fund the training and placement of these remarkable Great Danes with individuals who face mobility challenges, empowering them to regain independence and improve their quality of life. Thank you for being a part of this journey and helping us make a difference.

URGENT PLEA!

Thank You For Reading My Book!

Do you know anyone who is looking for some inspiration in their life? Be a friend, and give them the book that can help change their lives for the better.

Please take two minutes now to leave a helpful review on Amazon letting me know what you thought of the book.

www.ingramcontent.com/pod-product-compliance
Lightning Source LLC
Chambersburg PA
CBHW060141150626
46550CB00015B/2571